MARTINI

Alexander B. Struminger

TODTRI

M.Schiff

THIS BOOK WAS DESIGNED AND PRODUCED BY TODTRI PRODUCTIONS LIMITED
P.O. BOX 572, NEW YORK, NY 10116-0572
FAX: (212) 279-1241

PRINTED AND BOUND IN SINGAPORE

ISBN 1-57717-022-9

AUTHOR: ALEXANDER B. STRUMINGER

PUBLISHER: ROBERT M. TOD
EDITORIAL DIRECTOR: ELIZABETH LOONAN
SENIOR EDITOR: CYNTHIA STERNAU
PROJECT EDITOR: ANN KIRBY
PHOTO EDITOR: HEATHER WEIGEL
PRODUCTION COORDINATOR: ANNIE KAUFMANN
DESIGNER: THERESA IZZILLO

PICTURE CREDITS

"MARTINIS, MY DEAR ARE DANGEROUS. HAVE TWO
AT THE VERY MOST. HAVE THREE AND YOU'RE UNDER THE TABLE.
HAVE FOUR AND YOU'RE UNDER THE HOST." —DOROTHY PARKER

THE ULTIMATE COCKTAIL

The Martini is the ultimate cocktail. It is cool and clear. It is pure as liquid crystal. For many years, especially the post-Prohibition era of the '30s and '40s in America, the word "Martini" was synonymous with the idea of a cocktail. If you were offered a tray of cocktails at a party in that Age of Enlightenment, it was a good bet that you would see before you a glimmering array of small 2 ½ oz. stemmed glasses holding a cold elixir of gin and vermouth. Since then the Martini has become a status symbol—an accessory of power and an expression of style.

DRYER AND DRYER

In the post-war era of the late '40s and '50s the Martini became progressively dryer. In Hollywood the humor got dryer to match, and the Dry Martini became the calling card of the new Hollywood hero and heroine. In the business world the three-Martini lunch became the fraternal ritual, while at home it was the cocktail hour into which Dad and Mom escaped from the serious concerns of the adult world. In the arena of politics elder statesman like Churchill and F.D.R. armed themselves with the cutting edge of a Martini before engaging in the serious business of jousting for power.

*"Try it and tell me
how you like it. It's a hot Martini."*

NOT JUST A DRINK

The Martini is not just a drink: it is a statement of style and taste; it is a social form of iconoclasm and a shared savor of solitude. It is at the same time a veiled beauty and the bride stripped bare, for nothing could be clearer and yet, so mysterious. It seems therefore appropriate that the origins are obscured by the horizon of time and the story shrouded in myth and legend. America made the Martini famous and introduced the world to its mysteries. But France, Germany, England, and Italy have also laid claim to the invention of this most enigmatic of drinks.

THE PROSPECTOR:
A STORY OF RUGGED CONNOISSEURSHIP

California, 1870, the town of Martinez: a prospector on his way to San Francisco came into Julio Richelieu's saloon to buy a bottle of whiskey. In those days customers carried their own containers, which were filled from the bar's whiskey keg, and often paid with a gold nugget or a sack of precious dust. On this occasion the gentleman in question felt that his nugget was worth slightly more than the whiskey accounted for. He demanded his change in the form of a cocktail. The facile bartender mixed a concoction of Old Tom gin, vermouth, bitters, and syrup. His customer sampled the unusual beverage, smacked his lips with pleasure and asked for the name. "I call it the Martinez after the name of our town," replied the proprietor. Today the town of Martinez, California, proudly displays a memorial celebrating the birth of the Martini there . . . and lamenting the loss of the "z."

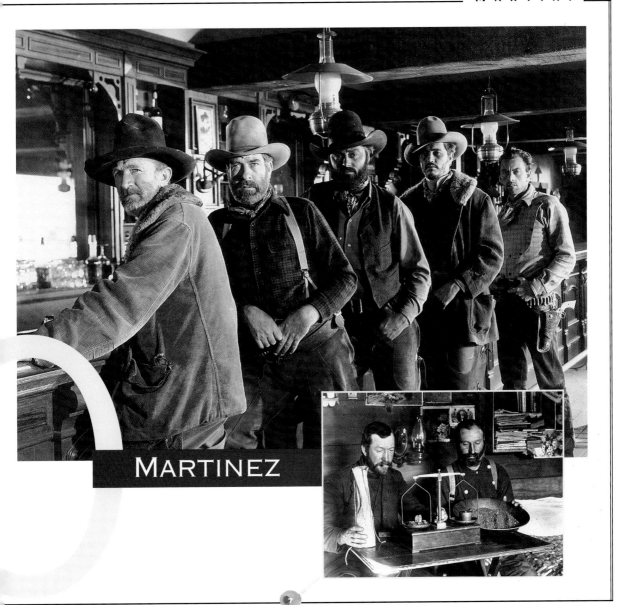

MARTINEZ

JERRY THOMAS:
A DOCTOR OF MIXOLOGY

Professor Jerry Thomas is perhaps single-handedly responsible for the popularity the cocktail enjoyed in America by the Golden Era of the 1890s. At least eleven editions of his book, *The Bon Vivant's Companion*, were printed between 1862 and 1934, and the work soon became regarded as the bartender's bible by every serious saloon or hotel bartender and amateur. It still ranks second only to the *Mr. Boston Official Bartender's Guide* in number of editions printed.

Mixing up a Blue Blazer.

THE BLUE BLAZER

In 1849, the young Jerry Thomas arrived in San Francisco Harbor on the bark *Annie Smith*, swept West by the romance of the California gold rush. He found a position with the Principal Bartender of the El Dorado Saloon, and soon came up with the flaming concoction of whiskey and showmanship called the "Blue Blazer," which would launch his career as an innovator and authority in the field of mixology. The Blue Blazer created a spectacle in the low lighting of the saloon as the flaming mixture poured back and forth in a wide arc between two silver mugs. It is reported that after the war President Ulysses S. Grant was so impressed by the Blue Blazer that he gave the Professor a cigar.

THE MARTINEZ, AGAIN

There is a story that in 1862 a fellow on his way from 'Frisco to that same little town called Martinez stopped into the bar at the Occidental Hotel, where "Professor" Jerry Thomas was the mixer in residence. It was an unseasonably cold day and this fellow asked the Professor if he could come up with something to bolster him. The man behind the bar spontaneously came up with a concoction astoundingly similar to the one in the previous story and named the new beverage "The Martinez" in honor of the customer's journey. It is reported that the man liked the drink so much that he stood at the bar all day and far into the night sampling the stimulating brew.

THE MARTINEZ COCKTAIL

(according to Jerry Thomas' recipe, not published until 1887)

Use small bar glass
One dash of bitters
Two dashes of maraschino
One pony of Old Tom Gin
One wineglass of vermouth
Two small lumps of ice

Shake up thoroughly, and strain into a large cocktail glass. Put a quarter of a slice of lemon in the glass, and serve. If the guest prefers it very sweet, add two dashes of gum syrup.

bon vivant

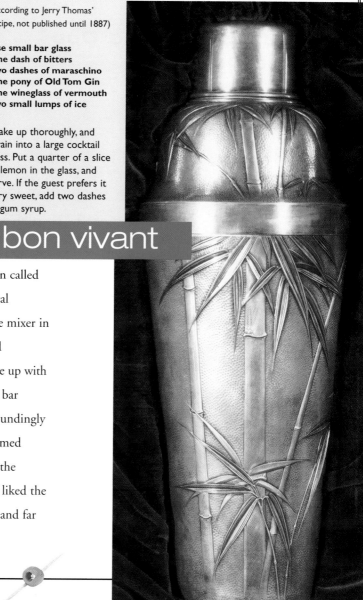

There's Something Odd in the Olive!

Shaking Up the Story

There's something odd in the olive here—two separate stories of the birth of the Martini (or, at least the "Martinez") are remarkably similar and, at the same time, just the opposite. Over and over, the one true original Martini is not easily pinned down . . . or, speared with a cocktail stick. Aside from the use of gin and vermouth (both were sickeningly sweet in those days), the Martinez only thinly resembles anything like what would be called a Martini nowadays. As we shall see, the road to the modern Martini is a stirring tale full of twists.

does indeed change, as
been seen in this detail
party at a seventeenth-
ury European pub.

A CHANGE OF TASTE

The 1890s saw the beginning of a taste for dryer cocktails. Although Jerry Thomas had earlier shown concern that the Martinez was not sweet enough for some customers, W. T. Boothby wrote in 1891, "[the Martini Cocktail] is made without any sweetening of any description, as the Old Tom Cordial gin and the

OLD TOM GIN

Italian vermouth of which it is composed are both sweet enough." This same decade also saw the adoption of dry French vermouth in favor of the sweet Italian. By 1919, the Old Waldorf-Astoria bar book held no fewer than three hundred recipes for mixed drinks, including a number of progressively dryer versions of the Martini.

INTERNATIONAL CLAIMS

THE GERMAN LEGEND

Several sources have upheld the claim of a minor German composer named Johann Paul Agidius Schwarzendorf (1741–1816). The story is that he had the nickname of "Martini" among his friends and invented two drinks that were promptly named after him. One (the important one) was based on a combination of Jenever and Vermouth—Jenever being that wonderful Dutch kind of gin also known as Hollands. From then, the new concoction was propagated by his friends and admirers, until eventually it made its way to the New World. In California saloons and New York hotel bars it found immense popularity and, finally, it flowed to the cosmopolitan centers of the world! One can find Schwarzendorf listed in the *New Century Cyclopedia of Names* (1954) as Jean Paul Egide Martini. He was born in Germany and journeyed to Paris where he changed his name to Martini and lived out his life as an organist and composer. That such a little-known figure could have had such a vast impact on civilization by the invention of a mixed drink boggles the mind indeed!

THE ITALIAN LEGEND

The Oxford English Dictionary credits the Italian firm of Martini and Rossi with the name for the Martini. Not surprisingly, this is a pedigree that those famous makers of vermouth have long nurtured. Certainly the ingredient of the Martinez and early recorded versions of the Martini was Italian sweet vermouth (dry vermouth was French and not commonly used in cocktails until the 1890s). According to Peter Tamony in the journal *Western Folklore* (1967), vermouth by Martini, Sola & Co., the predecessor of Martini & Rossi, had been available in American barrooms at least since the 1860s, and Martini & Sola had been exporting vermouth since 1834. Following the trend to dry Martinis in the 1890s, Martini & Rossi began to bottle a dry, or *sec*, vermouth as well. This implies another possible explanation for the ascendance of the name "Martini" over "Martinez"—the visual influence of the ever-present Martini name on the vermouth bottle.

Jenever

VINO VERMOUTH
Martini e Rossi-Torino

VERMOUTH BIANCO

AT THE
KNICKERBOCKER HOTEL

Two olives exchange a meaningful moment.

British cocktail pundit John Doxat tells the story of the Dry Martini with an Italian spin. The protagonist is Martini di Arma di Taggia, the Italian head bartender at the fashionable Knickerbocker Hotel in New York City, which just after the turn of the century attracted such regulars as the celebrated opera singer Enrico Caruso, who drank only fine French champagne, and the notorious oil tycoon John D. Rockefeller, who was a regular Martini drinker. Rockefeller's legendary stinginess was purposefully cultivated and publicized to the press, yet he always left a generous 25¢ tip. Martini's cocktail was the *Dry Martini*, a term he allegedly coined in 1911.

THE KNICKERBOCKER'S MARTINI

one-half London dry gin

one-half French (Noilly Prat) vermouth

dash of orange bitters

It was held to be a separate entity from then currently fashionable renditions of the Martini or the sickeningly sweet Martinez—a whole new approach that satisfied a different kind of taste and, as such, a whole new drink.

Martini di Arma di Taggia distinguished his approach from the simple gin-and-French that had already been popular in England and on the Continent for many years by stirring the ingredients with plenty of ice and then straining the drink into a chilled cocktail glass. Ice is, after all, a distinctly American contribution to the cocktail. Doxat adds, "some innovative customers took to spearing a green olive with a cocktail stick and putting it into their glass, a habit which bartenders later adopted." Although not nearly dry enough for modern tastes, this is a truly recognizable Martini.

Continuing the family tradition, John D. Rockefeller, Jr. (shown with financier Thomas Lamont) stands to drink a toast at the Waldorf-Astoria in 1941.

martini di arma di taggia

WHAT'S A COCKTAIL

NOT JUST DRY HISTORY

The Martini in name turns out to be a slippery quarry, but what about the Martini in fact? Nowadays, of course, we have coined the word "cocktail" generically to mean almost any mixture that can be served forth from behind the bar. This development may be a by-product of the term "cocktail hour" that came into popular use after World War II.

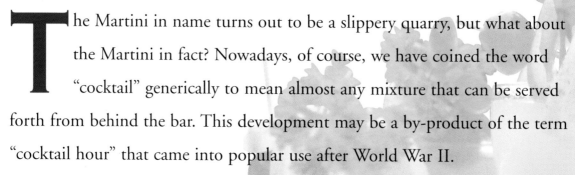

Certainly a great variety of mixed drinks of every sort have been served during that sacred hour. But in the early cocktail days of post-Revolutionary America there were only gin and brandy cocktails. In 1809 Washington Irving wrote in his *A History of New York*, "[New Yorkers] lay claim to be the first inventors of those recondite

beverages, cock-tail, stone-fence, and sherry-cobbler." Even the most astute student of the bar would recognize only the "cock-tail" from that list, but Juleps, Flips, Punches, Crustas, Slings, and Toddys also existed, or followed soon after. None of these was the same as a "cocktail." They were completely separate entities with completely different places in the pantheon of mixed drinks.

NOT JUST FOR BREAKFAST

As much later as 1862, the original edition of Jerry Thomas' *Bon Vivant's Companion* still lists only ten different kinds of cocktails, all of which were surpris-

ingly similar—a quantity of brandy or gin mixed with wine, bitters and syrup in some combination or other. "The cocktail," wrote Professor Thomas, "is a modern invention and is generally used on fishing and other sporting parties, although some patients insist that it is good in the morning as a tonic." At this time the cocktail was not generally served over the bar, but was a bottled tonic mixed specially for particular customers and often procured for trips into the country. Thomas' biographer, Herbert Asbury, tells us that as late as 1885 it had not become the standard before-dinner drink that it certainly was in the 1890s. The importance of the mixologist is apparent from the 1879 journal *Under the Gaslight*: "In the morning the merchant, the lawyer, or the

Methodist deacon takes his cocktail. Suppose it is not properly compounded? The whole day's proceedings go crooked because the man himself feels wrong from the effects of an unskillfully mixed drink."

"Auntie Mame" gets a light.

THE PROBLEM OF PROHIBITION

THE DARK AGES

In 1919 the Eighteenth Amendment to the United States Constitution passed, plunging America into a fourteen-year period of alcoholic darkness. Herbert Hoover proclaimed that Prohibition was "a great social and economic experiment, noble in motive." Equally noble in motive were the proliferation of speakeasies throughout the States and the determination of Americans

On January 12, 1922, police in Hoboken, New Jersey, raided 330 Court Street and seized the largest collection of moonshine apparatus ever taken in that state.

18TH AMENDMENT

to uphold their rights to the "pursuit of happiness." During this time standards of mixology reached an all-time low. Gin-slingers behind the speakeasy counter did not have the skill of the great bartenders of the Golden Age and had to work with poor quality spirits that rivaled those of the Civil War era for lack of scruple. The phrase "what's yer poison?" wasn't far from the truth.

Above: Drinking at the Speakeasy Bar. Right: Kentucky moonshine still in 1919.

WELL, MAYBE
JUST ONE MORE ROUND . . .

INNOCENTS ABROAD

In Europe fugitives from the cruel vagaries of Prohibition found solace in a well-made American-style Martini at the Ritz or Harry's Bar in Paris. In 1925 an intense literary rivalry began to flourish in Paris between two friends, F. Scott Fitzgerald and Ernest Hemingway. Doxat describes one occasion not long before the publication of *The Great Gatsby* and *The Sun Also*

Ernest Hemingway, left, F. Scott and Zelda Fitzgerald, bottom.

Rises. When Fitzgerald and Hemingway arrived at Harry's to meet Zelda Fitzgerald, she was drinking a new cocktail called the White Lady. "You wouldn't like it—it's sweet and delicious," Zelda told Scott. "Then I'll have a White Lady too," he replied, "for you are sweet and delicious." Ernest Hemingway was vaguely repelled by the sentimentality of the remark. He embodied the acerbic temperament of the new generation: "A Martini for me," he said, "and distinctly dry."

GOING FOR THE GIBSON, AND BEYOND

Meanwhile, not all Americans had succumbed to the sorry state of bath-tub gin and grubby speakeasies. According to Doxat, the renowned artist Charles Dana Gibson, creator of the Gibson Girl and a regular member of The Players (an exclusive New York speakeasy), once came into the club in an indecisive mood: "I don't know what I want, Charley," he said to Charley Connolly, the famous mixer behind the bar. He thought for a few moments. "Charley, make me a better Martini." Charley made a Martini, speared a pearl onion on a cocktail stick, and placed it in the glass. The subtle difference pleased Gibson and he asked to always have his that way. Hence, the Gibson.

THE END OF AN ERROR

REPEAL, WITH A TWIST

On December 5, 1933 the Eighteenth Amendment to the United States Constitution was repealed and the era known as Prohibition came to an end. On this great day an alarming discovery was made—there was no one around to mix the drinks! Over the fourteen-year period of the "Great Experiment" many of the great bartenders who knew the secrets of cocktails had retired or quit this world for the next, leaving no generation of young professionals to replace them. This was an especially stupefying problem for the grand hotels and restaurants, which now needed to

December 5, 1933: In the Casino Bleu at the Hotel Biltmore, a waiter mixes cocktails for one of the first repeal parties staged in New York City.

be prepared to serve alcoholic beverages with the same knowledge and authority that they affected in other arenas. Bartending schools opened up every-where, while publishers scrambled to find and piece together all of the turn-of-the-

GOOD OLD DAYS ARE BACK AGAIN!

> WE REJOICE, BACCHUS HAS RETURNED AGAIN,
> WE DRINK TO YOUR HONOR AND YOUR FAME
> WITH A TOAST TO YOU FROM YOUR CUP OF CHEERS
> THAT BANISHES OUR FEARS AND TEARS.
>
> —FROM *PIONEERS OF MIXING AT ELITE BARS*
> BY CHARLES C. MUELLER

THE GREAT EXPERIMENT

century recipes and wisdom that could be found.

AND THE WINNER IS . . .

When Prohibition ended, three mixed beverages had emerged as the definitive cocktails among sophisticates in America and Europe: the Manhattan, the Bronx (essentially a Martini with orange juice, reputedly invented by Johnnie Solon at the Old Waldorf-Astoria), and the Martini itself. Today many bars would lump these, as well as the Rob Roy and any other vermouth-based drinks, in the Martini family—while applying the word "cocktail" to everything else. The Four Seasons Hotel in New York—famous for its Martinis—does not disdain to put the Manhattan on its Martini menu and so enjoys the company of many followers of modern taxonomy.

Farewell Dinner

THE THIN MAN

The 1934 classic detective film *The Thin Man* (loosely based on the novel by Dashiel Hammett and starring William Powell and Myrna Loy as Nick and Nora Charles) illustrates the new flavor of the times. Powell is in an elegant club full of dancing couples, shaking a cocktail shaker in time to the music while surrounded by three attentive young bartenders. He instructs them: "The important thing is the rhythm. You always have rhythm in your shaking: the Manhattan you shake to the fox-trot, the Bronx to two-step time. The Dry Martini you always shake to waltz time."

"ONE IS ALRIGHT, TWO IS TOO MANY, AND THREE IS NOT ENOUGH."

—JAMES THURBER

STIRRED, NOT SHAKEN

Of course not everyone could agree on things like the rhythm of the shaking, even then! In *The Old Waldorf-Astoria Bar Book* (1934), "with Amendments due to the Repeal of the XVIIIth," Albert Stevens Crockett declares, "Modern practice prescribes shaking for a Dry Martini. This, however, weakens the mixture and used to be discountenanced by barmen who believe in tradition." This has been a bone of contention ever since. Most bar books that record mixed drinks of the Golden Age before Prohibition pointedly mention that of all the drinks, Martinis are always stirred. In his book *How to Mix Drinks* (1936) Bill Edwards makes clear that "certain cocktails such

A libation from *Gentleman's Agreement.*

mixed drinks

"Oh dear! You mean it should have been four to one the other way?"

as the Martini should not be shaken. The recipe says—STIR. Mix the drink in a bar glass half full of cracked ice with a long handled spoon, twirling and stirring it very quickly, then strain and serve."

Here are three progressively dryer Martinis from the pre-Prohibition years at the Old Waldorf-Astoria. All are STIRRED, not SHAKEN:

MARTINI No. 1

Dash of Orange Bitters

One-half Tom Gin

One-half Italian Vermouth (Stir)

Serve with a Green Olive

Twist piece of Lemon Peel on top

MARTINI No. 2

Two jiggers Gin

One-half jigger Italian Vermouth

One-half jigger French Vermouth (Stir)

Serve as above

MARTINI No. 3

(DRY)

Two-thirds Gin

One-third French (or Sec) Vermouth (Stir)

Serve as above

Even in this time when a dry Martini was a half-and-half, or a two-to-one at most, made with French vermouth, there were already a few apostles of the Dry Martini. Robert Benchley's dictum, which electrified early Martini-bibers was: three parts of gin and enough vermouth to take away "that ghastly *watery* look." Yet as the modern Martini began to evolve, certain hold-overs from the old recipes remained. Orange bitters continued to yellow some Martinis until World War II.

ALL SHOOK UP

SHAKEN, NOT STIRRED

On the other side of the argument, Harry Craddock, the famous bartender at London's Savoy Hotel, advocated shaking for all cocktails in *The Savoy Cocktail Book* (1930): "Shake the shaker as hard as you can: don't just rock it: you are trying to wake it up, not send it to sleep." By the end of World War II most Americans had adopted the European custom of shaking everything, including Martinis.

AN INTERNATIONAL AFFAIR

Everyone had an opinion on the proper way to make a Martini, and the world leaders of the day were no exception. Franklin Delano

Right: F.D.R., in a moment of relaxation. Above: his personal cocktail shaker set.

Claudette Colbert raises a glass to Gary Cooper in *Bluebeard's Eighth Wife* (1938).

SAVOY HOTEL

Roosevelt had a reputation for being a great enthusiast and a notoriously bad Martini maker. Reports indicate that he would put almost anything into his shaker and to the distress of his guests, into the Martini glass. However, he succeeded in entertaining Churchill, an avid drinker of Dry Martinis, and introducing Stalin to his first Martini at the Teheran conference. Stalin's comment was, "Very nice, but a little cold on the stomach." Reports of Churchill's sardonic approach to the Dry Martini vary from merely waving the vermouth bottle over the shaker to holding the shaker while bowing in the direction of France.

007

BY SPECIAL LICENSE

A discussion of shakers versus stirrers would be incomplete without a mention of the most famous shaker of them all. Nearly everyone of drinking age fondly remembers 007 striding confidently into the room (or falling through the skylight) with the words "Bond . . . James Bond" on his lips, to be followed closely by "shaken, not stirred." The proliferation of James Bond movies featuring the debonair Sean Connery ostentatiously drinking vodka Martinis (and bolstered by strong advertising campaigns by the likes of Smirnoff's) helped usher in the vogue

Sean Connery
as James
Bond in
Dr. No. (1962).

of vodka cocktails displacing gin as the liquor of choice—the *original* Bond Martini, however, contained gin.

In Ian Fleming's first full-length Bond novel *Casino Royal*, Bond orders a Dry Martini and describes his views to an accomplice: "I never have more than one drink before dinner. But I do like that one to be large and very strong and very cold and very well-made. I don't like small portions of anything . . ."

BOND, JAMES BOND

THE ORIGINAL BOND MARTINI

3 measures of Gordon's gin

1 measure of vodka (grain, not potato-based, if possible)

1/2 measure of Kina Lillet, shaken until ice cold

Serve in a deep Champagne goblet with a large, thin slice of lemon peel

MARTINI GOES TO THE MOVIES

MY MAN, GODFREY

David Niven as Oliv-or Twist . . . whoops! No, it's My Man Godfrey having a quick pick-me-up while no one's looking.

THE SNOWS OF KILIMANJARO

"I had never tasted anything so cool and clean . . . they made me feel civilized."

—Ernest Hemingway

Gregory Peck and company in *The Snows of Kilimanjaro*, looking very civilized.

"LET'S SLIP OUT OF THESE WET CLOTHES AND INTO A DRY MARTINI."

—ATTRIBUTED VARIOUSLY TO ALEXANDER WOOLCOTT, ROBERT BENCHLEY, MAE WEST, AND CHARLES BUTTERWORTH

ARTHUR

Sporting a very elegant shaker and shaking a not-so-elegant leg, Dudley Moore is the impossibly rich, possibly alcoholic, and quite spoiled star of *Arthur*.

DARK VICTORY

Nancy never let Ronald have so many Martinis—but then again, if he'd stayed with Bette Davis, he would probably never have made it to the White House.

A Toast to the Post-War Generation

THE RAT PACK

Although not movie stars, strictly speaking, Frank, Sammy, and Dean's adventure in *Oceans 11* proved that there was no racket they could be kept out of. The boys also had some real Martini experience, especially Dean, who as Special Agent Matt Helm tried to give James Bond and his "shaken, not stirred" thing some real competition.

HAPPY ANNIVERSARY

Martinus fidelus, or the Martini of Marital Togetherness. Nothing cements the relationship of long standing like a little oblivion (nice nails!). Notice the smaller size of the cocktail glass. The post-war generation certainly knew how to keep their Martinis manageable, and colder.

BEDTIME STORY

James Bond liked to drink his Martinis in Champagne goblets. Here Marlon Brando and Shirley Jones toast in the New Year while drinking Champagne from Martini glasses . . . wait a minute! Those are really Martinis. Now that's bringing in the New Year in style!

> "IF THE LORD HADN'T INTENDED TO HAVE A THREE-MARTINI LUNCH, THEN WHY DO YOU SUPPOSE HE PUT ALL THOSE OLIVE TREES IN THE HOLY LAND?"
>
> —FORMER HOUSE SPEAKER JIM WRIGHT

THE WAY WE WERE

Barbra Streisand demonstrates here that cigarettes (and not cigars) are the proper accompaniment to a Dry Martini. Robert Redford, as always, looks dashing and everyone looks, well . . . like they did in the '70s.

As Time Goes By

"Waiter, A Glass of Chardonnay"

ONE-MARTINI LUNCH

While the 1960s brought the Vodkatini, the '70s and '80s heralded a decline of the Martini in America. A new atmosphere of temperance that frowned upon such derelict social customs as the three-Martini lunch moved many people away from hard liquor. A fascination with things European helped supplant the Martini with wine and imported beer. That's alright, Martini drinkers abhor a crowd.

To appreciate the effects of the legends, apocryphal dictums, and ancient mystique on the Martini of today, one has only to look at the *Official Harvard Student Agencies Bartending Course* (1984). One will not find the Martinez, fortunately, but present are the Martini, Dry Martini, Extra Extra Dry Martini ("whisper vermouth softly over the gin"), 50/50, Gibson, Vodka Martini, and an example of modern ingenuity: the Tequini (Tequila Martini). All are garnished with olives and lemon twists. All are given with the following admonition, which is certainly a sign of the times: "Unless you work at a fancy bar, you probably won't make very many of these, but when you do they must be *perfect*. Martini drinkers are the fussiest people in the world. Be prepared."

THE RETURN OF THE MARTINI

The 1990s have ushered in a resurgence in the Martini's popularity. The modern Martini chic of Tanqueray's Mr. Jenkins, the Cosmopolitan, and the endless other new varieties based on creative combinations of liquors and vermouth substitutes, not to mention Gibson-style garnish variations: lime twist, anchovy or almond-stuffed olives, small green tomatoes, even baby shrimp . . . all have gone to revitalize the interest in the Martini. For these newcomers, as well as to purists who look with disdain upon the multifarious variations on the Martini theme, there is something mysterious and self-defining about the liquid in the long-stemmed glass.

DR. ROSOFSKY'S COSMOPOLITAN

The Cosmopolitan's all the rave
Its worldly wonders people crave
Their winter doldrums it helps stave
But really it's just after-shave

A few popular examples of the new breed of Martini:

THE COSMOPOLITAN

Vodka

Cointreau

Splash of cranberry juice

Lime juice

Served with a lime twist

THE METROPOLIS

Vodka

Strawberry liqueur

Champagne

THE CHOCOLAT-INI

Vodka

Creme de cacao

Served in a chocolate-rimmed glass

THE CAJUN MARTINI

Hot pepper vodka

Dry vermouth

Served with a jalepeño-stuffed olive

"Mr. Jenkins is encouraged that his suggestion to play 'no-handed pass the olive' is being received so enthusiastically."

MR. JENKINS

From prominent politicians to movie stars and literary lions, the cult of the Martini has had many heroes over the course of history. There are even fictional heroes . . . and as it happens, literature does not hold the monopoly! The cult of stardom of Tanqueray's Mr. Jenkins (or "The Jenks," as some fans affectionately know him) has spread from obscure curiosity to billboard adventures and even devoted home pages on the Internet—by sheer brunt of Madison Avenue will. Mr. Jenkins cuts a suave figure and may well perfectly embody the "retro-chic" of today's new generation of Martini drinkers. Purists, of course, will argue that there is nothing "retro" about Martini Chic. For them, as for us, the quest for the perfect elixir continues as before . . .

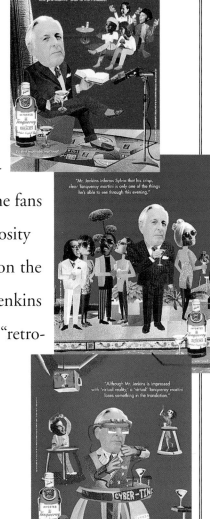

"Mr. Jenkins infuses the poetry reading with a new energy as he recites his turgid and provocative 'Ode to the Pimento'."

"Mr. Jenkins informs Sylvia that his crisp, clear Tanqueray martini is only one of the things he's able to see through this evening."

"Although Mr. Jenkins is impressed with 'virtual reality,' a 'virtual' Tanqueray martini loses something in the translation."

TALES FROM THE LOUNGE

A CLASSIC IN-AND-OUT

The most wonderfully ostentatious rendering of the "In-and-out" Martini I've ever witnessed went like this: The hostess poured an entire bottle of vermouth into a pitcher, then emptied it down the drain before refilling the pitcher with gin. "Just the right amount of vermouth!" she declared, filling our glasses with the contents of the pitcher.

Skyscraper cocktail shaker and glass, with Manhattan serving tray, c. 1938.

GATHER YE OLIVES . . .

At a party thrown by a New York publisher, I noticed a young intern drink one Martini after another while carefully setting aside the olives in an impressively growing pile. When I asked what he was doing, I was told that he was taking advantage of the opportunity to

special equipment one would use to freeze the gin . . . not to mention what happens to your tongue when you lick such a super-frozen treat.

A NOT-QUITE UNIVERSAL LANGUAGE

Over the years the search for the Dry Martini outside of cosmopolitan centers in European countries has provided many an obstacle for the Martini aficionado. While traveling in Austria, a friend confidently ordered a "*dry* Martini." After a quizzical look, the waiter retreated to the bar. Finally, he returned with the order. "Ein, zwei, *drei Martini*, bitte," he announced, as he lined up three glasses of Martini & Rossi sweet red vermouth before his astonished customer.

replenish his dwindling home supply of these important garnishes.

YOU NEVER FORGET YOUR FIRST . . .

Some believe that the alchymical marriage of gin and vermouth is evanescent. When at a recent party, someone suggested removing the ice and refrigerating a mixed pitcher of martinis, one guest declared that "you can no more refrigerate a Martini than you can a kiss."

THE MYTHICAL MARTINICICLE

I have never seen one, but I have heard tell of a most delightful sounding summer refreshment: the Martinicicle—frozen Martinis in ice trays with toothpicks. Although I can't help wondering what kind of

SEATTLE'S ANNUAL CLASSIC MARTINI CHALLENGE

Many of the most cultivated habits of cosmopolitan America have their origins in diverse places—but they are not usually called "fashionable" until they arrive in New York City. However, the 1990s resurgence of Martini chic was born not in the "sophisticated" East, but in the West-Coast cities of Seattle and San Francisco. It is only fitting that the West, from whence arrived the original—or, at least, the Martinez—should have incited this new era in Martini culture.

One of the main instigators of the '90s Martini craze is Seattle's Annual Classic Martini Challenge. Begun in 1992 as a showdown between five local Seattle bars to prove who mixed the best Martini, the competition is attended by aficionados from as far as San Francisco, home of a number of great Martini bars. The annual event is a gourmet's delight, featuring tournaments ranging from the best classic Martini to most creative, and the best Martini *hors d'ouvres* accompaniment. The contest is hosted by Oliver's at the Mayflower Park Hotel, which

Mike Rule, Oliver's winning bartender.

Above left: The Andaluca Restaurant at the Mayflower Park Hotel.

Above right: Oliver's, during the 1996 Classic Martini Challenge. Below right: And a fine time was had by all!

has annually taken the prize in at least one category, and includes such formidable challengers as the Four Seasons Olympic Hotel and the Metropolitan Grill. Some of the winning recipes may be found on pages 46-47.

PRIZE-WINNING RECIPES FROM SEATTLE AND . . .

2 1/2 oz. Bombay Sapphire gin or Stolichnaya Cristall vodka

1/4 oz. Cinzano dry vermouth

2 large vermouth-marinated Italian olives

OLIVER'S CLASSIC MARTINI

(Mike Rule, Oliver's in the Mayflower Park Hotel, 1996 Best Classic Martini)

•Start with an empty Martini mixing glass
•Pour 1/4 oz. Cinzano dry vermouth into the empty mixing glass

•Swirl to coat the inside of the mixing glass with the vermouth; dispose of excess vermouth in the sink
•Fill coated mixing glass with ice
•Pour 2 1/2 oz. of Bombay Sapphire gin or Stolichnaya Cristall vodka over the ice in the mixing glass
•Cap and shake vigorously
•Let the mixture stand approxi-

GLACIER BLUE

(Michael Vezzoni, Four Seasons Olympic Hotel, 1992 Best Specialty Martini)

1 1/4 oz. Bombay Sapphire gin

1 1/4 oz. Stolichnaya Cristall vodka

5 drops blue Curaçao

Orange twist, for garnish

•Fill a Martini mixing glass with ice
•Pour the Bombay Sapphire gin, Stolichnaya Cristall vodka, and blue Curaçao over the ice
•Stir briskly with a spoon for 40 revolutions
•Strain into an ice-cold Martini glass
•Garnish with an orange twist

AUTHOR'S NOTE:
Notice the presence of Cointreau and Curaçao in the place of vermouth in these modern variations. This kind of substitution is becoming more common as cocktail gourmands strive to increase the diversity of their Martini repertoire. The Four Seasons Hotel in New York

also uses Curaçao in their "Classic" Sapphire Martini. Diluting the gin with vodka, or just substituting, allows for a greater breadth of experimentation.

mately 20 seconds

- Place a set of large vermouth-marinated Italian olives on the edge of an ice-cold glass
- Strain the mixture into the glass over the olives

AUTHOR'S NOTE: *This is a variation on the classic "In & Out" favored by traditionalists from Auntie Mame to Kingsley Amis. I'm surprised that the Mayflower didn't hold out more firmly against vodka as a possible ingredient of the "Classic."*

FORTUNELLA
(Mike Rule, Oliver's in the Mayflower Park Hotel, 1996 Best Specialty Martini)

1/4 oz. Campari

3/4 oz. Caravella

1/4 oz. Cointreau

3/4 oz. Bombay Sapphire gin

1 oz. Ketel One vodka

1 tsp. candied kumquat nectar

1 lemon slice

Candied kumquat and lemon twist, for garnish

- Coat an ice-cold mixing glass with Campari and toss out excess
- Fill with ice and build with Caravella, Cointreau, Bombay Sapphire, Ketel One, kumquat nectar, and lemon slice
- Cap mixing glass, shake, and strain into an ice-cold Martini glass
  - Garnish with lemon twist and kumquat

THE AUTHOR'S MARTINI

A simple variation on the "In & Out." Add whole ice cubes to your pitcher or mixing glass, then the vermouth (I prefer French, if handy). Swirl the vermouth before straining off and adding a good Dutch Jenever. Stir until cold. Squeeze the oil from a lemon peel over the top of the glass (don't drop in!) and garnish with an olive.

EPILOGUE

Did the Martini really evolve from the Martinez? Was it merely the slurring of a "z"? One must certainly acknowledge the difficulty incurred when ordering a round of "Martinezes" . . . especially if it's not the first round of the cocktail hour! Although such etymological twists and chops do occur over time (Gin from "Geneva" or "Jenever" is a good example), the Martinez and the Martini may have evolved independently of each other. The truth is probably somewhere in-between.

Certainly there were a number of drinks technically no different from early Martinis in terms of ingredients with names that have been swallowed up by time, or cast aside by the vagaries of fashion. Of course none of these permutations comes close to the perfect Martini—the alchymical marriage of iced gin and vermouth that we have so laboriously pursued to perfection in the twentieth century. What will the next century bring? More of the same, we hope.

"Bartender!"